For a centur  than its fair ¦
quip on and
Mecca for L

to be a raucous, passionate and often rough and
ready following for whom the place for style and
sophistication was on the pitch. We've got it, too,
the Hammers are the home of football's skills'
academy whose roll of honour has included not
only three 1966 World Cup winners in Bobby
Moore, Geoff Hurst and Martin Peters but the silky
skills of Trevor Brooking, the goal-scoring talents
of Tony Cottee and the stylish tackling of Anton
Ferdinand. We have roared them to FA Cup and
European successes and when the team failed us
with relegation; we roared them back up to the top
division again. But no matter if it was cheers or tears,
the West Ham way was always the stylish way.

The Little Book of

WEST HAM

EDITED BY
ROBERT LODGE

CARLTON
BOOKS

First published by Carlton Books 2007

This book is not an officially licensed product of
West Ham United Football Club

Text and design copyright © Carlton Books Limited 2007

A CIP catalogue record for this book is available
from the British Library.

ISBN 978 1 84442 092 6

Printed in Singapore

❝ I'm forever blowing bubbles, pretty bubbles in the air. **❞**

West Ham's adopted anthem since the 1920s, taken from the musical 'The Passing Show of 1918'. Originally sung by fans in praise of Billy J. 'Bubbles' Murray

❛Rushes in where others feared to tread.**❜**

Club handbook assessment of
defender Walter Tranter, 1898

> ❛From the very first kick it was seen that there was likely to be some trouble. All attempts at football were abandoned.❜

The East Ham Echo *reports on an ill-tempered match with Millwall in September 1906*

'A notable amateur player who rejoices in the distinction of having been the only footballer other than goalkeepers to have worn spectacles in a professional football match. '

A 1947 history of West Ham recalls full back Stanley Bourne's claims to 'frame'

'Frequently there were suspicions of favouritism in their choices. '

*The **East Ham Echo** comments on directors handing over selection duties to manager Sydney King in 1908*

‘The best full back in Scotland.’

Manager **Syd King's** *assessment of*
new signing James Gault in 1907

❝ I was the best player Scotland
had on the field. **❞**

*Hammer **Jack Tresadern** reflects on his lack-*
lustre performance for England in 1923

> *On one side there was a back named Blackman who was a fair man and on the other there was a back named Fairman who was a black man.*

Athletic News *comments on multi-racial football at West Ham in 1910*

❝ I punched both goals into the net in full view of several opponents. **❞**

Danny Shea *makes Maradona's infamous 'Hand of God' incident look tame by coming clean about his goals in a fog-shrouded match against Nottingham Forest in 1911*

'Every vantage point was seized upon by spectators. Some climbed up the telegraph poles, others sat on top of advertising hoardings and looked every minute as if they would topple over. Round the banks there was one mass of humanity, packed like sardines in a box, but all as happy as could be. '

The **East Ham Echo** *report on the 1911 FA Cup visit of Manchester United to the Boleyn Ground*

‘The height of human happiness appeared to have been reached.’

*The **Morning Leader** reveals the joy of Hammer's 2-1 FA Cup tie win over Manchester United*

'Joy at West Ham as news was received that the club's application to join the Football League was successful.**'**

Athletic News, *1919*

He inspired the maxim "the bigger they are the harder they fall."

*Hammers trainer **Charlie Paynter** sums up Jack Tresadern's robust style of play in 1913*

' There are few goalies in the country who can hold and field a wet ball like him. **"**

*The 1920 **West Ham United Club Handbook***
entry for David Baillie who ironically played just
16 games for Hammers between 1925–29

> ❛The name of Gibbins is a household word in London football and it is to our great regret that he cannot assist us regularly for we would always find a place for him.❜

The West Ham United Club Handbook *of 1925–26 rues Vivian Gibbins remaining an amateur player and refusing to sign professional forms*

❝ He is a terror for his size. **❞**

A scouting report on diminutive George Horn, 1907

❝ I think it is a mistake to enter into a game with fixed ideas on tactics. **❞**

*Advice from utility player **Sidney Bishop**, 1926*

❝ I am too disappointed to talk; I haven't got over it yet. I want to forget it. ❞

*Manager **Sydney King's** reaction to West Ham's*
2-1 defeat by Bolton Wanderers in the first
Wembley Cup Final in 1923

❛I am not in favour with the change in the offside law. It has turned the game round and the team which can play kick and rush will nearly always win. This is putting a premium on those players who study the game from a scientific point of view. In fact, it robs the game of most of its science.❜

*Skipper **Billy Moore** is not happy with a 1924 change in soccer laws*

> **❝** Tremendously fast, at ball control he has few masters. **❞**

Journalist **Norman Ackland** *talks up winger*
Arthur Evans in 1930 but Evans featured
in only one league game

'Opponents learned to play James Ruffell the compliment of close marking; it was fatal to give him full rein to his exceptional speed and flashing shots.**,**

The verdict on the Hammers winger James Ruffell from the book **A Century of International Football**

❛West Ham went out of the first division
in an inglorious manner at Stamford Bridge…
it was hard to realise from this exhibition
that this was one of the most vital matches
in the history of the club.❜

Journalist **Charles Buchan** *on
West Ham's relegation in 1932*

'I most sincerely think Syd Puddefoot is the best centre-forward the world has ever seen.**'**

West Ham trainer **Charlie Paynter**
on his star striker of 1922

❝Tom could pick a fly off Vic's eyebrows.**❞**

*Manager **Charlie Paynter's** enthuses about*
winger Thomas Yews' pinpoint crosses to
centre-forward Vic Watson in 1923

‘This was not a match, it was a walkover.’

*The **News Chronicle's** verdict on the Hammer's 6-0 trouncing of Preston North End in September 1933*

'We players quietly split up and went straight back to our service units. '

Ted Fenton's *anticlimax after Hammers won the Football League War Cup, 1939*

> ❝ He was in his own half when he received the ball but a combination of swerve and speed took him right through the defenders until he had only the goalkeeper to beat and he equalised. ❞

The Times' *account of the first of Joe Foxall's five goals in matches against Spurs during the 1938–39 season*

‘ West Ham will commence the season under ground difficulties. **,**

*The **Stratford Express'** coded way of saying a German rocket had hit the Boleyn Ground in 1944*

> **❛** The lights seem to make the game look faster. It was like watching a fantastic ballet in glorious Technicolor. **❜**

Newspaper report on Upton Park's first floodlit match in April 1953. (The Hammers also wore fluorescent shirts)

'He should be revered. They should have a statue for him at West Ham. He laid the foundation for the success of the club – not for what he did on the field but the knowledge he gave to other people.'

*West Ham player **John Cartwright's** praise for 1950's teammate Malcolm Allison, credited by many as the founder of the West Ham 'Academy'*

> ❝I'd been a professional for two and a half months and Malcolm had taught me everything I knew.❞

Bobby Moore's *tribute to his mentor Malcolm Allison*

❝ I should never have left West Ham. **❞**

*Winger **Harry Hooper** rues his parting in 1956 despite a later successful career with Wolves and Birmingham*

❛ Keep forever asking yourself: "If I get the ball now, who will I give it to?" **❜**

Malcolm Allison's *advice to the burgeoning talent that was Bobby Moore*

'The selection of Bobby Moore at left half proved justified by a display which foreshadows a grand future for a 17-year-old called upon to make his debut against one of Europe's leading sides. '

Hammers match programme on Moore's appearance against Manchester United in 1958

'When Moore was on his way in, we thought he was a bit slow but we knew he was going to be a good player. '

Vic Keeble, *West Ham centre-forward of the 1950s and 1960s*

❝ George Fenn is the most exciting prospect in the country and I expect him to be the cream of the crop. **❞**

*Manager **Ted Fenton's** usually excellent eye for a prospect failed him in 1958. Fenn failed to make a first team appearance*

'We won the (FA Cup) Final and we won in Europe. Few sides in those days, other than the top clubs, could dominate. '

John Lyall *on the successes of the*
1964–65 Hammers team

❝ It was the way we won, for me
it was fulfillment. **❞**

*Manager **Ron Greenwood** after the European Cup
Winners' Cup victory over TSV Munich in 1965*

He is a player's player – a tremendous worker but people do not appreciate his value.

Geoff Hurst *on midfielder Ronnie Boyce*

'West Ham 4, West Germany 2. '

*The **Stratford Express'** verdict on the England's 1966 World Cup win. (Geoff Hurst's hat-trick and fine performances from Martin Peters and Bobby Moore sealed a historic victory)*

> ‘The English Di Stefano.’

Ron Greenwood *compares winger Johnny 'Budgie'*
Byrne with Real Madrid's star winger of the 1960s

"I must have played with Bobby Moore more than anyone else. I often thought "He's gonna miss this," but he hardly ever did."

*Fellow defender **Ken Brown** was alongside Moore as he developed into a world talent*

❝The coming of Byrne was a great thing in my career. He and I worked up a great partnership as the team began winning. I was perfectly happy to be the bread and butter part of the partnership. I rate Budgie as the best player I have ever played alongside.❞

Geoff Hurst *reveals in 1964 his admiration for strike partner Johnny Byrne*

> ❝At West Ham you could play blindfolded, we played to systems. At Manchester United there was no coaching. We played off the cuff. There was little in the way of team playing.❞

Full-back **Noel Cantwell** *rated the Hammers' academy above the Old Trafford regime of the 1960s*

❝ I am looking for someone big and strong and not afraid to work. **❞**

Ron Greenwood *tells Geoff Hurst why he was converting him from half back to a forward in 1962*

❝ Ron Greenwood turned Geoff from a bit of a carthorse at wing half into a truly great forward. None of us thought Geoff was going to make the switch. It took him years of hard work and patience but he was so willing he ran himself into the ground. **❞**

Bobby Moore *on Geoff Hurst's role change in 1964*

‘There are two people in my life that are real heroes. One is Lester Piggott and the other is Ron Greenwood. Ron stimulated my brain so much in terms of football, more than anybody. ’

John Bond *puts his own managerial successes down to Greenwood's advice*

❝When training, Oxo is the only beverage used by our team and all speak of the supreme strength and power of endurance which they have derived from its use.❞

Sydney King *reveals the 1904–5 team's sports drink of choice.*

❝ I sorted out the team formation last night lying in bed with the wife. When your husband's as ugly as me, you'd only want to talk football in bed. ❞

Harry Redknapp *the realist*

❝ Geoff Hurst was a bloody cracker of a player. **❞**

Centre-half **Ken Brown's** *praise for his striker teammate*

‘The best soccer show seen in London for years. ’

*The **London Evening News'** verdict on a titanic clash with Spurs which the Hammers won 4-3 in November in 1966*

‘I just want you to know that I want to stay at West Ham and help get the team back to the First Division. ,

*England star **Trevor Brooking's** words to manager John Lyall moments after the Hammer's relegation in 1978*

❛In other people's eyes he was a most underrated player but to us he was invaluable, The thing that impressed me most about his play was his ability to do the simple things quickly and efficiently. **❜**

Ronnie Boyce comes in for high praise
*from **Ron Greenwood***

❝ Even when they had Moore, Hurst and Peters, West Ham's average finish was about 17th, which just shows how crap the other 8 of us were. ❞

Harry Redknapp *pulls no punches*

‘ 10 years ahead of his time. **’**

How England Manager **Sir Alf Ramsey**

rated Martin Peters in 1966

❛When I left West Ham to go off and coach, Ron told me all I needed was a good memory. He said: 'If you remember all the things we've done together, you'll be all right.'**❜**

John Bond *recalls Ron Greenwood's advice*

' Have I got anything bad to say about him? Well, he got cautioned by the referee at Burnley once. '

John Lyall *recalls in his book* **Just Like My Dreams** *how Trevor Brooking had erred*

❝ If I have a serious falling out with the board that calls for my departure I will leave the club in probably the healthiest state it has ever enjoyed. ❞

Harry Redknapp *in 1998*

❝ You've got to give him a great deal
of the credit for what he did. **❞**

*Everton manager **Walter Smith** on Paolo Di Canio who*
had caught the ball rather than score in an empty net
when he saw the Everton goalkeeper lying injured

'He floats like a butterfly – and stings like one**'**

Brian Clough *on Trevor Brooking in 1980*

‘ There was competition for Trevor Brooking because he was hot property. **’**

Ron Greenwood *recalls Brooking's*
early days in his team

> He was always recognisable as an outstanding talent; a gifted player and an exceptional individual. Even from the early days you could sense he had a tremendous career ahead of him.

Bobby Moore *speaking of Trevor Brooking*

❝ Alvin, Alvin Martin, he's got no hair
but we don't care. ❞

Fans' chant *for the popular defender during the 1980s*

'West Ham was always regarded as a family club; I had two managers in 19 years. '

Trevor Brooking

❝ Not being able to watch the great man at first hand was perhaps something I lost out on. Mooro left the club a few months before I arrived. ❞

Alvin Martin *on Bobby Moore*

❝ The supporters at West Ham were marvellous; they always encouraged forward and midfield players to be creative. **❞**

Geoff Hurst's *tribute to West Ham's fans*

❝ Looking back when I first started off, the big worry was if I was going to make the grade. **❞**

Trevor Brooking

‘The John Lyall team of the early 1980s, led by Bill, was probably the most enjoyable era of all… three Wembley visits in quick succession and a European campaign to boot.’

Alvin Martin *reflects on the West Ham team skippered by Billy Bonds*

❛ If a member of the family is in trouble,
you look after them. **❜**

*Hammers Manager **Alan Pardew** on Shaun
Newton's ban for taking drugs in July 2006*

❝ I'm seen as a role model to young children and that is what makes it so bad. I've let down my family, my friends, the club and its supporters. **❞**

Shaun Newton *on his cocaine shame*

❛Everybody deserves a second chance – and to be fair he seems a lot calmer than Tomas Repka!**❜**

Alan Pardew *on signing Moses Ashikodi in 2006*

❝ He led with his head, he didn't head-butt. **❞**

Alan Pardew's *explains a player's*
misdemeanor in 2005

> **'** We signed to play until the day we died, and we did. **,**

*Former Hammer **Jimmy Greaves** speaks on radio, not from beyond the grave*

❛Julian Dicks is everywhere. It's like they've got 11 Dicks on the field. ❜

Metro Radio

I don't like people who drain my time and energy. If you've seen the Harry Potter films, we use the term 'dementors' – people who can draw the life out of you in terms of your energy. So we eradicate the 'dementors', encourage the positive people, and that spreads around to create the team spirit we have here.

Alan Pardew

❝As soon as I did it I realised what I'd done. I'm not the dancer – I'm usually the bloke at the bar.❞

Alan Pardew *on being seen on TV touchline dancing in delight*

'Swerving the ball inside the defender to the near post was something we worked on a lot at West Ham; it produced a lot of goals for us. '

Bryan 'Pop' Robson's *tribute to Trevor Brooking's skills*

‘ Simplicity is genius. **,**

Ron Greenwood's *simple philosophy*

‘ I enjoy big games and I usually win them. **’**

Alan Pardew *before the Hammer's*
appearance in the 2006 FA Cup final

❝ I fell backwards and it went towards the goal. There was no question of guiding it. **❞**

Trevor Brooking *on a rare headed goal*
that won the 1980 FA Cup final

It's almost like he has Dr Who's Tardis because he always turns up on time.

Alan Pardew *on Teddy Sheringham*

❝ He put West Ham on the map. **❞**

Hammers' Chairman **Terry Brown's** *tribute to Ron Greenwood after the former manager's death in 2006*

'Our famous academy may have been formed in the late 1950s but it was Ron Greenwood who developed that approach and took it to the next level. He changed the status of the club from a small family, parochial outfit to an internationally recognised brand. '

West Ham Match Programme, *March 2006*

❝ Liverpool came down on one occasion and won 3-0 at Upton Park. By the time Ron had dispensed his wisdom to the media many a report read that Liverpool took the points but West Ham played the football. ❞

Sunday Times' *sports journalist* **Rob Hughes** *recalls Ron Greenwood's legendary post-match briefings with sherry*

❝ When collectors buy the programmes from the respective FA Cup successes of 1964 and 1965, they are preserving the success brought about by Ron Greenwood. ❞

Match programme tribute following the death of the former manager in 2006

" Bobby Moore was the best defender
in the history of the game. "

*German captain and legendary
defender* **Franz Beckenbauer**

‘ Confidence is all important in this game and
I am very positive in this direction. ,

Defender **Anton Ferdinand** *on receiving the Barclays*
Premiership 'Player of the Month' for February 2006

' I can understand the club's reaction but I was still genuinely upset and disappointed to lose two roles within the club that have been dear to me. I am really sorry that the news came out when it did and I accept that it was not in the best interests of the club. '

Tony Cottee *on the fall-out from his reported takeover bid at Upton Park*

❝ There is pressure on you whenever you put on a football shirt to try to put in a good performance. ❞

Teddy Sheringham *on playing*
Premiership football for West Ham aged 39

❝I'm delighted for Alan because its all too easy to sack a manager when the fans are getting on his back but West Ham stuck with him and they are reaping the rewards.❞

*Commentator and former player **Alan Brazil** on the board's support for Pardew when Hammers promotion push was flagging in 2005.*

'Sometimes in your footballing career you have to seize the moment.'

1980's defender **Tony Gale's** *philosophy*

❝ Glen Hoddle hasn't been the Hoddle we know. Neither has Bryan Robson. ❞

A strangely convoluted match commentary extract
*from the usually-erudite **Ron Greenwood***

❛I don't know the Spanish for "on me head, son" but I'm working on it.❜

Alan Pardew *works on the language barrier after the signings of Argentinians Tevez and Mascherano*

❝Bad results slaughter me, they gut me.**❞**

Harry Redknapp *didn't like losing*

'He chanced his arm with his left foot. '

An anatomically challenged comment

from **Trevor Brooking**

‘ A wonderful player; a wonderful
gentleman of sport. ,

*A fan's tribute to **Bobby Moore** upon the
former Hammer's death in 1993*

❛ I've just been given a video recording
of the game and I'm going to tape
"Neighbours" over it. **❜**

Harry Redknapp *was not happy with West Ham's*
goalless draw with Southampton in 1995

'Without doubt this is my worst season as a manager. I don't know where the next goal is coming from '

Manager **Harry Redknapp** *in 1997*

> **❛** I am an accountant and I'm very suspicious of everyone in football. **❜**

Hammers Chairman **Terry Brown**

‘They can make any one look good. I signed Marco Boogers off a video. He was a good player but a nutter. They didn't show that on the video.’

Harry Redknapp *on videos promoting possible new players and the infamous signing of Marco Boogers*

'I will always be remembered as the player who cried at Wembley! When I was collecting my winner's medal there were tears in my eyes. Most West Ham fans I speak to still recall it vividly. And they always mention the moment I was brought down by Willie Young. It is the first thing they remember!'

Paul Allen *recalls his record-breaking appearance in the 1980 FA Cup Final*

'Football is a simple game. The hard part is making it look simple.**'**

Ron Greenwood

❝ You're not a real manager unless
you've been sacked. **❞**

Malcolm Allison, *who was to have been dismissed
several times in his managerial career*

'He was the Fagin of the penalty area, the arch pickpocket of goals.

*Sports writer **Geoffrey Green** on the skills of Jimmy Greaves*

❝The whole thing had hurt him, which was understandable. He gave the impression of being a hard man but he was quite sensitive and I know he was very worried about the effect it would have on his family.❞

Ronnie Boyce *recalls the Lou Macari betting saga*

‘I was crazy to resign like that because, looking back, and knowing what football is like today, I suppose it really was no more than a storm in a teacup. ’

Lou Macari's *hindsight on his resignation*

I found it hard to believe how the club could employ someone who had gambled against his own team and I just found it impossible to play for him.

Mark Ward's *verdict on Lou Macari*

❝Losing means a very bad Saturday night. It is like a personal injury, like something has gone badly wrong in your life.**❞**

Harry Redknapp *on defeat*

'Jimmy Greaves used to hang around like a substitute best man at a wedding for 85 minutes and still win more matches than any other player. '

*Sports writer **Ian Wooldridge** on Greaves' match-winning abilities*

' Up the 'ammers! **'**

The regular cry of **Til Death Us Do Part** *sitcom character and diehard West Ham fan,* **Alf Garnett**

❛John Bond has blackened my name with his insinuations about the private lives of football managers. Both my wives are upset.❜

Malcolm Alison *in joking mood*

' Geoff has a hammer in his left boot and good left feet are like bricks of gold. **'**

Jimmy Greaves *praise for teammate and prolific goalscorer Geoff Hurst*

❝ As I was heading towards goal, Alan Ball was shouting: 'Hursty, Hursty give me the ball!' I said to myself: 'Sod you Bally, I'm on a hat-trick'. ❞

Geoff Hurst *recalling his memorable third goal in the 1966 World Cup final*

'By the look of him he must have headed a lot of balls.'

Harry Redknapp *on Iain Dowie*

❝ Playing with wingers is more effective against European sides like Brazil, than English sides like Wales. ❞

Geography may not have been
Ron Greenwood's *strong point*

❛ Harry, we've decided to let you go. **❜**

*Chairman **Terry Brown** gives the bombshell news of his sacking to Harry Redknapp who had been expecting an improved contract*

❝ When I see all my legs out, I have confidence. I look at my muscles and they look big and I feel strong. With big shorts, I can't see my muscles at all. **❞**

Paulo di Canio *on why he wore*
unfashionably short shorts

‘Bobby Moore was great at that. Someone would come and kick a lump out of him and he'd play as though he hadn't even noticed. But 10 minutes later... whoof! He had a golden boy image, Mooro. But he was hard. ’

Geoff Hurst *on club and country skipper Bobby Moore*

❛He was the first gentleman of football for me.**❜**

Ron Greenwood *singles out Trevor Brooking*

> To find a way past Bobby Moore was like searching for the exit from Hampton Court Maze.

Sports writer **David Miller**

❝ Billy used to start training in the gym an hour before everyone else and I used to do the same in the hope of being as fit as he was. He was first class and the type of person who you wanted to play for. ❞

Mark Ward's *admiration for*
Billy Bonds' work ethic

‘I remember Wembley,
When West Ham beat West Germany.
Martin one and Geoffrey three,
And Bobby got the OBE!’

*A popular West Ham terrace chant following
England's 1966 World Cup win.*

‘The rules of soccer are quite simple, basically it is this; if it moves kick it. If it doesn't move, kick it until it does. ’

Hammers' Welsh international **Phil Woosnam**

❛I enjoyed centre of midfield best. I was at my peak playing there in the early 1970s. My best years were definitely spent in midfield. I could run all day and I was physically powerful. I could influence games from there and I thought I did at times. I absolutely loved that role.❜

Billy Bonds *on his preferred position*

❝It really did look as though not one person had left. They got me to do a lap of honour. It was an emotional night, a wonderful send-off and I could not have wished for better.**❞**

Trevor Brooking *recalls his last First Division match against Everton in 1984*

❝ I've already had three or four of our players on the phone. They are all very excited by the news. **❞**

Alan Pardew *reveals he has his players backing on the signing of Tevez and Mascherano in 2006*

❝ I'd love to know who it was because I am going to cane the life out of them! **❞**

*Striker **Bobby Zamora** finds his teammates' appreciation of the two new Argentinians hard to take*

> ❝McAvennie played football for a living. Pretty good he was at it as well, achieving legendary status at West Ham in a striking partnership with Tony Cottee.❞

*Striker **Frank McAvennie** recieves high praise for his achievements at Upton Park from a Celtic fanzine*

I never enjoyed management. It was a way of staying in the game. But, for me, it could never replace playing.

Billy Bonds *on management*

' I think the world of John Hartson. **,**

Manager **Harry Redknapp** *backs his erstwhile striker following Hartson's conviction for kicking flower baskets around a shopping mall in 1998*

‟It was nothing.”

*Another defence of Hartson by **Redknapp** after*
the striker's headline-hitting training ground bust-up
with Israeli international Eyal Berkovic in 1998

❝ What he did was totally out of order. ❞

Harry Redknapp *rethinks his earlier comments*
on the Hartson/Berkovic clash

❝It was just frustration. When I speak to West Ham fans now and I bump into people on holiday they just tend to remember the bad things. What people forget is the incredible time I had before that.❞

John Hartson *on the Berkovic incident*

'After you've scored a goal it's just orgasmic... if you asked me just after a game I'd says its better than sex, but if you asked me just after sex I'd say "forget it, mate". ,

*Winger **Trevor Sinclair** on scoring – one way or the other*

"Once he had the ball, you beware. He could make you look a fool in one moment."

Arsenal goalkeeper **Bob Wilson** *was ever wary of Trevor Brooking*

The thing about sport, any sport, is that swearing is very much part of it.

Jimmy Greaves, *West Ham United 1970–71*

There's no spark. The squad is hopeless.

Harry Redknapp *on the Billy Bonds team of*
1992–94 relegated twice in three years

❝The crowds at West Ham have never been rewarded by results but they keep turning up because of the good football they see. ❞

Ron Greenwood

Football tactics are rapidly becoming as complicated as the chemical formula for splitting the atom.

Jimmy Greaves *reflects on the changing game*

❝ When you are a scorer, the public judge you on how many goals you get rather than on how well you are playing and that's just another pressure you have to learn to live with and cope with. ❞

Bryan 'Pop' Robson

‘ My schoolboy hero was Bobby Moore. I have never had another one, partly because I outgrew the age of hero-worship and partly because no one since has measured up. ,

Best-selling author **Sebastian Faulks**

‘Those in football should make the
bucks while you can... if there is a chance
to earn a few quid, take it because
it doesn't last forever. ’

Harry Redknapp's *financial advice for players*

‘He is the untidiest man I know. People don't believe me because he always looks so immaculate. ’

Hilkka Brooking *lets some of husband Trevor's domestic secrets out of the bag*

❝I've not renewed my season ticket, because I'm not going to give the directors my money. F*** them!❞

*Actor **Ray Winstone**, plays the*
upset Hammers fan in 2004

❝ If I could I'd like to sit down with every West Ham fan and explain my decision. ❞

Joe Cole *talking about his move to Chelsea in 2003*

❝The passing of two of their former managers, Ron Greenwood and John Lyall, has left great gap in the game. Both men were responsible for leading the Hammers into the modern era.❞

*FA Chairman **Geoff Thompson** mourns the loss of two great West Ham managers in 2006*

❝ If Lyall had told us what he was going to do, it might have upset our rhythm. ❞

*Midfielder **Geoff Pike** on John Lyall's last-minute*
'secret' lone striker strategy that won the 1980 FA Cup

‘We must never lose the history of the club.’

Alan Pardew's *pledge as takeover bid*
rumours grow in the summer of 2006

❝ It's very difficult to say why we've been so successful in youth terms; I suppose it's down to a number of factors but, most importantly, our recruitment area of east London and Essex is really fertile. ❞

Tony Carr, *West Ham's Director of Youth Development*

‘To see opposing captains Nigel Reo-Coker and Steven Gerrard squaring up today is a wonderful snapshot of England's future.’

Sir Trevor Brooking, *FA Director of Football Development, reflecting on the 2006 FA Cup Final line-ups*

‘The lads put in all the effort and I get the goals. I'm loving it.’

*Striker **Marlon Harewood** top scorer in Hammer's 2006 FA Cup run*

> ❝The West Ham fans have been good to me,
> i had no problems with them.❞

Jermain Defoe *on his £7m transfer to Spurs 2004*

'This next batch of kids won't go the same way as the last generation. ,

Terry Brown, *West Ham Chairman*

‘He was my friend as well as the greatest defender I ever played against. The world has lost one of its greatest football players and an honourable gentleman. **▮**

Pelé's *tribute to Bobby Moore*

❝Our fans will contest every tackle, win every header and make every save with us.❞

Alan Pardew's *tribute to loyal Hammers' fans*

Thanks

Cassell's Book of Sport Quotations
West Ham United, An Illustrated History by
John Northcutt and Roy Shoesmith
Just Like My Dreams by Trevor Brooking
A Century of International Football 1872–1972
Morley Farror and Douglas Lamming
Broken Dreams by Tom Bower
Days of Iron by Brian Belton